5 Minute Mastery™

The Surprising Secrets for Transforming Your Stress to Success and Mastering What's Important

GRANT PARK PRESS
6350 LAKE OCONEE PKWY, STE 110,
#74 GREENSBORO, GEORGIA 30642

ISBN#
978-1-7325527-0-8

Dedication

To my wife Vicki and daughter Jennifer, who have supported me on my journey while I was developing my 3-step formula for completely transforming people's lives.

Rave Reviews of
5 Minute Mastery™

"Read this book if you want to achieve success and have more balance at work and at home."
– **Jack Canfield**, Coauthor of the *Chicken Soup for the Soul®* series and *The Success Principles™*: How to Get from Where You Are to Where You Want to Be

"***5 Minute Mastery***™ provides a great perspective in gaining your best self in all that you do. John captures the essence of how energy allows you to gain your flow of leadership. I truly appreciate what he has provided as a guide for leaders."
– **Dr. DeRetta Rhodes**, Executive VP & Chief Human Resources Officer YMCA of Metro Atlanta

"In this book, John Fenton reveals simple to use secrets that anyone can follow to manage stress and be a better leader."
– **Wayne Berson**, CEO of BDO USA, LLP

"***5 Minute Mastery***™ will inspire and empower you to live your life by design. Intellectually, understanding mastery is simple, but learning to embody mastery takes effort. John Fenton lays out the process for anyone to follow."

– **Gary Strack**, former CEO of Orlando Health

"Implementing the strategies in ***5 Minute Mastery***™ gave me the ability to at least double my writing production within the first week of using them. John J. Fenton offers a practical system for increasing mental focus and clarity."

– **Colin J. Campbell,** Copywriter, Formula Marketer™

"If you're looking for ways to gain more clarity, freedom and success, look no further than John Fenton's ***5 Minute Mastery***™."

– **Marci Shimoff**, #1 NY Times bestselling author, *Happy for No Reason* and *Chicken Soup for the Woman's Soul*®

Hold on!

Make sure you check out the **FREE BONUSES** that come with this book. ***5 Minute Mastery***™ comes with a series of bonus material (a real value: $297):

- (3) Downloadable "Five-Minute Shift" Audios you can use to get grounded, focused and energized.
- Video Training: "How to Close The Awareness Gap™: Keys to Team Self-Esteem in Business."
- Bookmark with all "8 Principles of Successful Company Culture."
- Application for John J. Fenton to coach you or your team.

Get Access Now At:

https://www.johnjfenton.com/book-free-gifts/

TABLE OF CONTENTS

Introduction

Could it be possible for anyone to sustain peak levels of performance, without compromising their health and sanity?

If you're an executive or businessperson with a schedule packed with responsibilities, you know what it's like feeling constantly stressed, overwhelmed and overworked. The nature of the business world is so focused on the future that it's easy for us to forget about what's happening now. We're almost always thinking something along the lines of "What's happening next? Which *list items* can we check off? Which *actions* will help us meet our quarterly and annual goals?" "What *tools, tactics, or resources* do we need to achieve the results we planned for?" The worry. The stress. The anger and frustration. The quiet desperation. It's not easy. If the demand for your mental and emotional energy has ever made you feel like quitting, you are not alone. If the pressure at work is becoming so great, the rewards no longer seeming worth the effort, I understand how you feel, and it is my intention to give you tools and insights you can use to re-energize your life with a new sense of purpose and fulfillment. With this new sense of purpose, you'll achieve higher levels of performance at work, while protecting you from physical, emotional and mental burn out. You'll find your *center*; that place in your mind that transforms workplace chaos into clarity, focus and confidence. You'll find yourself being a better leader – conveying a sense of certainty to the people around you without needing to say anything. Your employees and team members will give you their trust, respect, and effort. You'll run a tighter ship and feel great about it.

There's one more benefit that comes from mastering the strategies I'll share with you: **financial security and independence.** When you're a highly productive leader, you are never out of a job. You're so valuable to the success of an organization that you simply cannot be replaced. That type of security results in providing your family with the lifestyle they deserve; the lifestyle you deserve.

That may sound like a tall order.

It may even sound *too good to be true*.

However, the reason I can make these promises to you is because I've been where you are and have made it to the other side. On the next page, I'd like to share my personal story with you. You'll learn exactly how I overcame burnout and regained balance in my personal life – while simultaneously leading the transformation of my company's culture and productivity. After that, we'll explore ways for you to do the same. Are you ready?

1

How I Overcame Corporate Burnout & Discovered the *Secret* to Sustainable Energy

As a managing partner with BDO[1] I was responsible for a team of approximately 60 people who maintained consistent growth, year after year. We took on all sorts of new work in a competitive and complex market, and enjoyed growing our company exponentially. In addition to managing our team, I had my own client responsibilities and book of business to take care of. There were weekend meetings and conference calls, sometimes on Saturday nights, and the time-commitment was taking over my life. I

---

[1] BDO, USA, is a member firm of BDO, a global accounting and consulting firm made up of an international network of public accounting, tax, consulting and business advisory firms

remember returning home late one night after being with a client, working on a project that meant hundreds of millions of dollars to his company. My wife, who was normally very supportive and understanding, had reached her limit. She was standing in the driveway in a tearful rage, pounding her fist on my car, screaming, “Why aren't you home!? Why aren't you ever home!? All those countless 80-hour weeks... Guilt and shame... Neglecting my family... Anger and fear... A never-ending cycle of pressure and tension... All those things were eating away at my personal life like a disease.

My team felt it too. Weeks full of tension would build up and I’d suppress my anger and frustration. At some point, the feelings would boil over and I’d snap at someone for the smallest thing. People in the office started avoiding contact. They found it hard to share valuable information with me because they feared how I might react. To add salt in the wound: I felt like I *should* know how to solve these problems. I read *all* the professional development books and went to *all* the seminars. My library is packed full of *how to* material. Why couldn't I get this right!? The sense of tension and guilt was building up. I knew the solution was not in more "how to" information. Another time-management course was not going to help me. I knew I'd find my answer *somewhere else*.

Discovering Sustainable Energy

Being a productive person in the business world does not mean you have to sacrifice health, family time, happiness or sanity. There must be a solution. Something kept telling me there must be a way to create a balance, without needing to compromise my level of performance. So, I searched for answers. The journey led me to a midtown office building, two blocks from my office. I walked through the lobby and noticed a big sign that said *Yoga and Tai Chi.* I walked into the center and met with a young Korean gentleman dressed in all black. I said, "Well, this is not my idea of yoga." He laughed. We sat down to talk. As we were talking, I looked up and noticed a big banner on the wall that read, "Tai Chi: The Way to Limitless Energy. Find Your Center." That resonated with me. So, I opened my wallet and paid him for personal one-on-one morning sessions. Over the course of just over a year, I trained with him almost every week. When I couldn't show up to the studio, we met over Skype. When we couldn't meet over Skype I practiced on my own. Within that year+ of practice, hard work and discipline I earned my black belt in Tai Chi.

The result of all that practice was that I got my life back. The business world was the same; busy, crazy, fast-paced and competitive. But I had changed. I could transform the stress into clarity and focus, while remaining calm and grounded. Work stayed at work. I no longer carried a cloud over my head at home. I could finally be present with my wife and daughter. I also started earning more money. See, discovering how to assemble my life within a context of self-care and mental focus gave me the ability to manage my team in a way that ended up making us one of the top 10 offices within the firm.

The shift was so significant in my office that people started noticing a difference – about me – and making comments. I started leading more authentically. This shift in my leadership, I believe, played an important part in the culture of our company.

The morale kept growing with our people. The relationships within our organization grew stronger. Our company culture began transforming from “every person for themselves” to “every person for each other.” The higher-trust culture gave our employees a sense of pride and they took greater responsibility in their work. They started leading themselves. They didn’t require micro-managing. They took on more tasks and completed them efficiently. The shift that I was experiencing internally and the knowledge I was gaining in my practice of Tai Chi was creating amazing results.

Some people may read my story and think, “So, you’re recommending I spend the next year+ of my life becoming a master of Tai Chi?”, and the answer is: no. It’s not necessary. See, I wanted to turn my experience into something I could share with others – something people could easily understand and implement in their own lives. My original misconception about these skills was “*this stuff takes too much time*.” But it doesn't have to. No matter how busy your life is you can use this material. I will not ask for much time from you. For instance, the first tip I'll share with you only takes 5 seconds.

I also understand you may have your own ideas about topics like mindfulness, Tai Chi, yoga, and other spiritual practices. So, I will not speak about those things. Instead, what you'll get is a practical, straightforward approach for taking control of your career and personal life. I'm going to summarize my experience and share it with you in three simple moves.

Firstly, you'll learn how to ***Energize*** your body and mind. As a result, you'll be in the best position to make critical decisions in business and personal life. Take my example for instance: as I was mastering the ability to create, sustain and manage my energy, the strategic decisions I made in business became easier. Where, before, I often felt uncertain and even downright afraid to make a decision due to fear of making the wrong decision, or worse, from exhaustion. Most of us know what our options are. However, what we struggle with is which option to choose *for us!* So, the strategies you'll discover in the *Energize Phase* will give you both physical energy and mental/emotional confidence. Also, it's important to know that *Energize* will be the majority of the focus within this book because it is what I see most businesspeople need most; a process to get reconnected with their best selves, and it is the foundation for greater success. In other words, giving you more *stuff to do* isn't my intention with this book. Secondly, in the ***eXecute Phase*** you'll learn success strategies you can implement and eXecute immediately with your team for higher morale, productivity and leadership. These mindsets are some of the most powerful tips I've picked up over my life. They will help you turn the knowledge from this book into habits that stay with you. The final step you'll discover is more of a *result* that happens by applying the first and second steps. The third step is to ***Empower*** your life. Meaning, you're going to create a life by your own design, instead of feeling like you're constantly reacting to the urgent stresses. You will feel empowered and that will transfer to the people around you.

In summary, the three steps you'll discover in this book are: ***Energize*** your body and mind, achieving vision and clarity for you to... ***eXecute*** the most important priorities that move you closest to your ideal results and finally... ***Empower*** your life by YOUR design. I refer to these three steps as the "*EXE Formula*" and I've spent years of my life simplifying and refining the knowledge you'll discover here. I will share the *EXE Formula* in the clearest terms I know how, and this will reduce the time in your learning curve. The best part is you are not required to *do* more in order to get results. Instead, my three-step formula is about *optimizing* what you're doing now, becoming more *conscious* of your actions, and reducing the amount of resistance and attachment involved in each moment. I understand time is your most precious resource. That's why my top intention for this book is helping you free your mind from mental and emotional burdens so you can successfully simplify your life.

Phase One: Energize

12

Get in Touch With Your Heart

Some people – especially men in business – are uncomfortable talking about things like energy, intuition and spirituality. They tend to write those topics off as *woo-woo* or *nonsense*. They typically say, "Just show me the technique!" Businesspeople often *think* they need more strategies, tactics and systems to succeed. But more *doing* has a way of detaching us from our heart.

Our heart is like a GPS that guides us in our life. If we are disconnected from that source, it inhibits our ability to make higher-level strategic decisions. During an interview with one of my mentors, Jack Canfield, co-author of the *Chicken Soup for the Soul® series and The Success Principles™*, I asked him what he thought was the most important skill a person could develop in their life. We laughed together as he said: “We need more woo-woo!” I couldn’t agree more.

The Day My Heart Stopped

Tuesday, September 25, 2012, after hosting a weekend retreat and hiking to the top of Stone Mountain near Atlanta, Georgia, I went to the doctor for a routine checkup. Thirty minutes into the checkup, the doctor rushed in and told me to “Lie down! I’m calling an ambulance!” The next thing I know, I’m in the ambulance racing across town, my heart beating at an uncontrollable rate, the lights flashing and the siren screaming. For me, everything seemed to slow down. They rush me into to the cardiac ward of the hospital, and the next thing I feel is the cold operating room table on my back. The doctors and nurses are looking at me worried. I thought "Why are you looking at me!? I don't know what is happening! I don't know what is wrong with me! Am I going to die!? Is this it!? Is this the end!?" All I could think about was my wife, my daughter. I had a flashback of my daughter when she was 3 years old standing on our stairs saying, "Catch me daddy, catch me!" I almost missed. I took a breath and a sense of peace and calm and clarity came over me. "I'm not ready to go. I have more to give, more to love".

A voice said, "His heart is..."

Everything went black.

Time suspended.

Nothing.

Just darkness.

I gasp for air and open my eyes. My mind is foggy. I can barely see. I don't know what is going on. I'm in the recovery room and Vicki is holding my hand, fighting back her tears and says, “Your heart stopped. I thought I had lost you. I love you.” I love you, too, I said. I asked the doctor, “Am I going to be okay?” He said, “You’re stable now.”

He went on, telling me about how my body was in virtually perfect condition. They had no idea why my heart wasn’t working properly. They did all sorts of tests for blockages in the arteries and other tests. This crisis was a *mystery*. Days and weeks went by and still no answer. While at the hospital my heart had quickly normalized and I was sent home after a couple of days. Doctors told me to take it easy for a couple months. It was that day in the hospital when I decided to follow my passion and create the peace and clarity that I had felt in those minutes when I faced death. I vowed to create peace and clarity each and every day of my life.

If you've experienced a serious health challenge, you know how sobering and frightening it is. You're forced to confront your own mortality and the things you value most are put into question. You begin considering things and thinking about things in a new way.

To me, there was no mystery in what caused my heart to stop. It was a sign that I needed to shift my life's purpose. It was a way of my spirit saying, "John, you've accomplished every goal you've set in the corporate world, but your heart is somewhere else." Eight months after my "heart crisis," *as I like to call it,* I left my position at BDO and became a full-time coach and trainer, helping executives and businesspeople increase their productivity while achieving more fulfillment in their personal lives.

The Source of Your Intuition

I tell people my wife did a great job of raising our daughter. In 2009, a movie came out called *Where the Wild Things Are.* It is based on a children's book. When my daughter (who is now 34) saw the preview she said, “Oh, I love that book!” I never knew she even had that book. Probably one of the biggest regrets is not having had the freedom to spend more time helping her when she was growing up. I think it’s because I wasn’t really connected to my heart. So, as we progress on this journey, I invite you to get in touch with your heart as much as possible. Allow yourself to feel. Listen to that small voice that tells you which moves you need to make for you and your soul’s expansion.

18

The 5-Second Shift

As a leader, *everything flows from you.* Your thoughts and feelings, whether spoken or unspoken, are unwittingly transmitted to the people around you. Thoughts and feelings are a form of energy. They're intuitive and subconscious, and they resonate like waves of sound or light. The difference is we cannot hear or see them, but we can *sense* them. Our thoughts and feelings either attract or repel people. If our energy is depleted or drained, that's what we communicate to the people around us.

Whether you're a solo-preneur or you run a company of 10,000 people, you need to be able to transfer a sense of calm to the people around you. You need to be able to *energize* yourself – fill up your cup – before you engage with your team. That's what the

Energize process is all about. It's about taking control of your energy so that you can gain the personal benefits, and also transfer it to the people you surround yourself with in your life. So, be prepared to feel differently and have that impact those you surround yourself with.

Breathe (in the air)

The *Energize* process begins with probably the easiest technique anyone can learn. We're all born with this ability, yet few of us maximize it. The first technique is simply becoming conscious of your breath. If you recall the story of my experience in the hospital, I took one final breath before everything went black. Years later, as I thought about that experience, I realized that breath could have been my last. Thankfully it wasn't. It was actually the beginning of a new chapter in my life. It's the same for everyone.

It's important to understand and really appreciate this simple truth...

***Any breath* could be our last, and *every breath* is a chance for a new chapter in our lives.**

In the time it takes to take a breath, everything – I mean *everything* – can change. Breathing is the only autonomic function in your body you can take conscious control over. Think about it. The other functions that regulate our body are basically out of our control: heart rate, digestion, urination, pupillary response, and even sexual arousal are things we can't alter. However, breathing is something we can consciously alter. We can take a shallow breath. We can take a deep breath. We can take a giant gasp and fill our lungs in a second. We can also practice taking slow and steady breaths and fill our lungs over 30 seconds. Aside from a health related ailment that physically prevents us from breathing, we have complete control.

Our nervous system has an innate *fight-or-flight* response that can get triggered. When you breathe deeply, you're stimulating your sympathetic and parasympathetic nervous systems, giving you more conscious control of those triggers. When you exhale through your mouth, you're releasing your stagnant energy and the tension in the body. Actually, in an article by the *Times of India* entitled *Advantages of Deep Breathing Exercises,* the author points out deep breathing also helps our physical body in the following ways: It's a natural painkiller, improves blood flow, increases energy level, reduces inflammation, detoxifies the body, stimulates our lymphatic system, and even improves digestion. Aside from the physical benefits we can gain from consciously controlling our breath, it's the easiest way for us to tap into the present moment and shift our psychological, emotional and spiritual state. Most of the time, we're stuck in our heads, analyzing and calculating the future or the past. We're not in the present moment. When we breathe consciously, we get connected to our body.

Your body is always in the present moment.

Our minds can always drift off into space, thinking about the past and the future, but our body is always in the present moment. Try it for yourself now. Bring your awareness to the physical sensations on the top of your head. You'll likely notice how the thoughts fade into the background for that brief moment. You're connected to those physical feelings in the present. Now, take a deep breath. Notice how the feeling of breath brings you right into *The Now*? There's no grasping, no worrying, no strategizing, and no attachment. It's just a feeling of your body in the present. From this point forward, think of your body as a vehicle into the present moment. The gas in that vehicle is the air you breathe. The more you become aware of your breath in every passing moment, the more grounded and present you'll be in those moments. That's the first fundamental you need to understand about getting grounded and transferring a sense of confidence to your team. This moment, right now, you have the ability to turn a new chapter. Remember: your body is the vehicle back to the present moment and your breath is the fuel. The more you can focus on your breath, the more present you become. The more present you are, the more powerful and energizing you are to the people around you.

Breathe.

The Triangle of Energy Flow

There's a certain way energy flows in our body. There are several pathways in our body and the major energy pathway is at your spine. It flows up your spine to your head, and it comes down the front of your body, down to your lower abdomen, in a big cycle. When we're under stress, energy gets blocked. Sometimes it's in our head, other times it's in our chest (like mine was), other times it's in our throat or other places. For clarity and focus, we need to bring the energy down to our lower abdomen. Think of it like a triangle. When we're in our head, thinking all the time, attempting to control the future (or worrying about the past), it's like that triangle is upside down with the apex at the bottom and the base at the top. All the energy is at the top. It's also unstable. You have to balance that triangle on the point at the bottom. Most of us are trapped in that inverted triangle. We spend our whole life from the head down. However, when we stay in touch with our body, it's like flipping that triangle around to its proper balanced state with the wide base on the floor. Now we're stable, grounded and connected. The further we can extend that base into the ground, and the wider we can send it out, the more grounded we become. As leaders, we need to create that stability in ourselves in order to transfer it to others. If you extend that triangle further from your energy center down to your feet, you're creating a wider triangle. You're creating this stable base and grounding yourself energetically. With this flow, you're releasing stress from your upper body as you exhale. You're also circulating refreshed energy through the rest of your body as you inhale. That has a tremendous power to shift your state. It also enhances your ability to think accurately and avoid emotional hijacking. When you are that calm state, you are tapping into your best self. You're making better decisions. You're more focused and clear-headed. You approach communication and relationships with ease and understanding. The way you lead is from a place of grounded calm, instead of frantic reactions. This is actually the mechanism through which you can sustain peak levels of performance. Sure, your energy will ebb and flow, and there will be times when you feel like you don't have any energy left. That's when you can make the shift and energize yourself.

Master the "5-Second Shift"

Remember: any breath could be our last, and every breath is the chance for a new chapter in our lives. The *Energize* phase begins with perhaps the easiest technique in the world for greater productivity: one breath. If you're in a stressful situation and your brain is beginning to feel like it's about to explode: take a single, deep breath. Allow that breath to be the trigger for change. Take one, then another and another. Allow it to cleanse your mind. That breath only takes 5 seconds, but it can place in motion a whole new experience for the moments that follow. Instead of feeling *reactive*, you can choose to be *active* and *responsive*. The more you practice this, the more habitual it becomes. The more you practice, the more the *Power of Accumulation* takes hold and your clarity becomes more natural and easier to achieve. Read more about the Power of Accumulation in the *Empower phase* later.

The 5-Second Shift is a Trigger

You can use the *Five-Second Shift* (one single breath) on its own. However, I encourage you to use that first breath as a reminder to take five minutes to truly get grounded. Obviously, the title of this book is ***5 Minute Mastery***™: taking five minutes to regain your posture and energizing your body and mind, in my opinion, is the minimum amount of time to create a significant shift.

Imagine your mind is like a crowded restaurant full of people. You hear the conversations, the laughter, the music, plates clanking, and maybe even the distant sound of the chef and kitchen crew. It's a busy place with lots going on. Now imagine a pin dropping in that room. Everyone continues talking and going about their business. You, however, are the only one who can hear the sound of the pin on the floor. Everything else, all the insanity, fades off into the background. The busy environment is like all the voices and imagery bouncing around in our heads. It's very chaotic. The pin dropping is like the first breath we take. It's gentle and small. Yet, we have the power – through our consciousness – to place more attention on that breath than the chaos. You can choose to turn your breath into a *trigger* to transform all the internal noise into focus. Then, turn that trigger into something that lasts at least five minutes, where you consciously apply different techniques to the breath, body and internal thoughts.

You'll notice, before we transition to the *eXecute Phase* I provide you with three different "5-Minute Shift" exercises that you can use at any time to energize yourself. The first *5-Minute Shift* is what I call *Getting Grounded.* It is focused on bringing your energy down to your feet and directing your power toward your body instead of your mind. It also prevents you from "giving your energy away." The second *5-Minute Shift* is called *Energizing Your Body.* It is especially useful for times when your physical body is feeling drained, or when stress is building up in your body. The third *5-Minute Shift* is called *Your Best Self.* It's useful for letting go of guilt or shame. For example, you may have made a tough decision that didn't produce the results you wanted and you're beating yourself up for it, second-guessing yourself over and over.

All three *5-Minute Shift* exercises have been tested by me for over 10 years with the CEOs, executives and business-people I've mentored. Many of those men and women send unsolicited testimonials to me about how the exercises have given them the calm they need while in the middle of the craziness of their work and their lives. Also, in the *Additional Resources* of this book I am including the audio files of all three of the following *5-Minute Shifts*. Before we get started, please understand that you cannot get a *5-Minute Shift* wrong or right. If you keep thinking, “Is this working?” then you’re thinking too hard. Use these techniques to bring your awareness into the present moment. Trust what you feel in your body. If you don’t feel anything, that’s okay, keep doing the exercises. They’re working just the same.

5-Minute Shift: *Getting Grounded*

Sit in a chair with your feet flat on the floor. I recommend you take your shoes off but you don't have to. You want to feel the floor with your feet, and more specifically, feel the balls of your feel. Gently press the balls of your feet into the floor.

Stretch your arms out and move your neck from side to side, loosening and stretching out any kinks. Relax your shoulders. Relax your chest.

Imagine a string at the top of your head stretches your back up, maintaining a straight spine.

Rest your forearms on your legs with your palms facing upward.

Relax, and even smile a bit. Enjoy the pleasant sensations of your body as it rests. Scan your body and notice any tension or pain. Relax further.

Become aware of your breath.

Breathe in through your nose, way down to the bottom of your stomach.

Exhale through your mouth and feel your body relaxing. Feel your shoulders, neck, underarms and arms release. Release your spine, your hips, even your legs, your ankles, and your feet.

Become conscious of the surface of your skin from the bottom of your feet to the top of your head.

Keep your attention on the pleasant sensations associated with your breath; both the feelings of expansion and compression when you inhale and exhale.

Focus on the physical sensations through your body and feel a deep sense of relaxation and calm. Also, notice the quality of those sensations; do you feel warmth?, Tension? Tingling? Heat? Cold? Numbness? No quality?

Be here.

Be right in this moment.

Continue breathing and maintain your attention on your body.

Now, every time you exhale, imagine that air going all the way down through your feet and into the ground beneath you.

First, focus the air to the immediate feeling of your feet touching the floor. Then, see if you can send it even deeper, as if every exhale were sending roots from your feet into the ground.

Expand the base of that ground connection to either side of your body. Widen the connection. Imagine that *Triangle of Energy* getting stronger.

Now, while maintaining your focus on your breath, the ground and your body – invite yourself to be grounded. You may even say that in your mind, "I am grounded." Feel the bottom of your feet.

Continue that cycle for as long as you like: breathing, connecting with your body, focusing on your connection to the ground, and saying “I am grounded.”

Whenever you’re ready, redirect your attention to what is happening in the room you’re in. Take a big breath and signify this new moment.

How do you feel?

Do your best to maintain that shift in feeling from this moment going forward.

5-Minute Shift: *Energizing your Body*

Sit in a chair with your feet flat on the floor. Stretch your arms out and move your neck from side to side, loosening and stretching out any kinks. Make sure your spine is straight.

Relax shoulders.

Rest your hands on your knees, palms facing up.

Make sure your feet are flat on the floor. Feel the soles of your feet.

Focus on your breath.

Breathe in through your nose and gently and slowly exhale through your mouth.

In through your nose.
Out through your mouth.

In through your nose.
Out through your mouth.

Do this for 10 breaths counting backwards from 10 to 0. One inhalation + exhalation equals one breath. So: A breath in and out is 10. The next breath in and breath out is 9. The next breath in and breath out is 8, and so on.

Now place your palms on your lower abdomen, right below your navel. That is your *Energy Center* and it's also a key acupressure point.

Keep your attention on your lower abdomen. Continue breathing. In through your nose and out through your mouth.

Focus on the feeling in your body as your abdomen expands and contracts, breathe in, and breathe out gently.

Now, raise your hands off your knees and face your palms toward each other about an inch apart. Imagine that, between your palms, you’re holding a plate.

Begin rotating your palms in circles as if you're cleaning the plate.

Continue maintaining the awareness of your breathing and your body. However, keep rotating your palms and focus on your palms.

You may begin feeling sensations between your palms, like a small ball or balloon, maybe you feel some heat or warmth or maybe some tingling. Use your breath and your imagination to grow and expand that ball.

The deeper you breathe in and out, the greater the ball of energy grows. The greater the ball grows, the more relaxed you feel and deeper your breath becomes.

Continue doing this for one to three minutes. Then, slow down until a stop, and hold your palms there facing one another.

Again, relax your shoulders and keep your spine straight. Breathe in through your nose and out through your mouth.

Now, bring your hands closer together. Move them as close as you can without touching. Imagine you're holding a ball or a balloon. Focus entirely on your palms, between your palms, and the golden ball of energy, the degree of energy. Make it denser and stronger. As you exhale, feel the energy between your palms. Slowly bring the energy ball back to your lower abdomen, just below your navel. Feel the sensations in your body.

Now you can move your hands to your knees, palms facing up. Breathe in, breathe out. Bring your consciousness back to your surroundings.

One more time: breathe in and breathe out.

You’re complete.
Now, with your palms nice and warm, you can massage your face, like you're washing your face. Sweep down. Sweep your shoulders.

5-Minute Shift: *Your Best Self*

Place your feet flat on the floor. Straighten your back upward and take a nice long breath into your lower abdomen.

Take one long breath in through your nose, hold, and let it out through your mouth.

Allow your shoulders and neck muscles to relax. Enjoy the pleasant sensations of relaxing your body.

Breathe in through your nose, and out through your mouth.

Take 10 long breaths like that.

Now, focus on a moment in your life when you may not have been at your best. Maybe you got angry or frustrated and said some things you didn't mean – some thing or action that looking back on it, you regret.

When you have that image or that thought, what were you feeling? What words describe what you felt in that moment?

Search your feelings.

Whatever words that come up are okay. Just allow the words to come into your mind.

Now, I'm going to give you an imaginary pen and imaginary paper. (You can do this on imaginary paper or actually write the words out on a piece a paper. Either method is effective.)

With your imaginary pen and paper, write those words down. Write all those feelings in that moment. Now crumple that paper up. Hold it in your right hand. Now we're going to let go of those negative words.

Hold the paper up.

Now you have an imaginary match in your left hand. You're going to light that paper and let go of all those negative words. On a count of three, 1 – 2 – 3! Release!

Now relax. Those words are not you. They're just feelings. Maybe they served you at one point. However, you have finally outgrown them and deserve to replace them with more supportive feelings.

Bring your hands back to your knees now. Breathe in through your nose, exhale through your mouth.

Breathe in, and exhale.

Now, picture a moment in your life when you really felt like everything was flowing, when you felt you were at your *Best*. Everything was just working. It doesn't have to be a big home run or big event, but something in your normal day-to-day life. You felt really complete. You were focused. Imagine that moment.

What words describe how you felt in that moment? How did you feel?

What are some other words that you felt? There are many, many, many more words that you could probably come up with.

I'm going to give you another imaginary pen and a piece of paper. Holding the paper in your palm, write those words out describing how you felt in that moment. Take that paper in your right palm and press it into your chest, into your heart. Feel those words in your heart.

How do you feel now?
Stronger? More capable?

How much stronger do you feel now compared to how you felt with the words that you just let go of a moment ago?

Note the shift. Allow the shift to stay with you. Return to that state, that *Best Self State* any time you need to rekindle your sense of courage and self-reliance.

Phase Two: e**X**ecute

How to Transform Energy into *Momentum*

If you'll recall, the *Energize Phase* was all about energizing your body and mind so you can achieve vision, clarity and focus. With that energy and focus, you're able to optimize how well you ***eXecute*** the most important priorities in your business. Earlier, I mentioned the majority of the contents in this book would be focused on the *Energize Phase* because it's where I've found that most executives and business people like you need help (as opposed to giving you more tactical *how to* material that fills up your plate and adds to your to-do list). In the many programs, seminars and retreats that I create for my clients, I design a customized set of activities and exercises for my audience that teaches leadership practices, business-building and team-building tactics and strategies in addition to the physical, mental and emotional techniques I've guided you through so far. If you would like to learn more about which programs could benefit you or your company, head over to the *Additional Resources* and find out the different ways I can support you beyond your time reading this book. Having said that, in this section in the *eXecute Phase,* I'd like to share with you some of the most useful knowledge I've gained about the topic of mindset, teamwork and leadership. The tips I'll share will help you collaborate better with your team, get more done in less time, and create a high-trust, high-productivity company culture. We begin with what may be the single most important mindset any leader needs to master.

It's called...

50

Outdoing by Out***being***

As a kid, I always felt like I wasn't good enough. I was 30 pounds overweight, kept my head down, and tried my best to stay hidden. I felt ashamed; shopping with my mom in the "Husky Department" at the local Sears Department store. The kids at school were cruel, picked on me relentlessly, and I didn't even stop them. I was raised in a mid-sized suburb of south Florida called Hialeah. Football is important to the people who live there. Having a child that plays collegiate and especially professional football is one of the most common aspirations and it's very competitive. But I hated sports because I could never do well at them. The more people talked about football the worse I felt about myself. My mom was concerned with my weight. She also wanted the kids to stop picking on me. She figured the best way to do that would be to enroll me in Optimist Football (little league football in our community back then). She did enroll me and I resisted. I couldn't play football! I couldn't do what the other kids could! I didn't feel worthy. Plus: I hated the process of having to practice.

Optimist Football had categories for both age and weight. I was too young to play with the kids my size and too big to play with the boys my age. So after a week of whining, complaining, and being kind of an ass, my mom said, "OK, you don't have to go back." Looking back, I now realize that I was infected with *victim consciousness*. Secretly I admired the boys who played football. I really did want to be good like them, I just felt like *I* wasn't good enough. So I never tried.

The Green Wall

Then, something happened that turned everything around... The President's Physical Fitness Award was a big thing in the U.S. in those days. The sixth grade was the first time we were exposed to all the physical tests. I failed miserably. I couldn't pull myself up the rope. I couldn't do anything. Fast-forward to junior high school, we had physical education every day. The coach ran it like a platoon with four different groups. These four groups of boys represented their level of performance the previous year in the President's Physical Fitness Award. Each group wore a different color shirt. The top performers wore gold tee shirts. The next group wore blue, then red. Everyone left over wore white tee shirts.

Can you guess which shirt I wore?

Yes: white.

Coach made us run a mile around the field to warm up. I'd run way in the back of the pack; whining, moaning and complaining – "why are we doing *this*?" After the mile warm-up, we then ran through an obstacle course. It was like being in the Marine Corps. We had all these different obstacles to climb under, over and around. Finally we got to the end and there was a big green wall. For the life of me, I could not get over that wall. It seemed really big to me then. When I tried to climb over the wall and couldn't, Coach said, "Just forget about it, Fenton. Go around!"

One day, the entire group was gathered on part of the track. A boy in a gold tee shirt walked up to us kids in white tees and said: **"You guys are a bunch of creampuffs!"** and the rest of the gold tees laughed. For some reason those words punched me right in the gut. It made me angry, yet it resonated with me at the same time. I went home, looked in the mirror and said to myself, “That’s not me. That’s not who I am.” I knew I could do better than I had been. So I made the decision that, from then on, I would run at the front of the pack. I promised I wouldn't complain or whine any longer. I made a promise to myself I was going to conquer that entire obstacle course and make it over that green wall. That moment was the biggest turning point in my life. In that moment, I went from having a *Victim’s Consciousness* to a *Master’s Consciousness* (which I’ll explain deeper in a moment).

The obstacle course was visible from my house. I saw it every day from my front yard. On weekends, I practiced running through those obstacles. I kept thinking and feeling what it would be like to win the gold tee shirt and the Fitness Award. I kept thinking what it would feel like to make it over that green wall. That’s exactly what I did. Later that year, I made it over that green wall and earned myself a blue shirt. The gold shirt was within striking distance. It was the next year that I even won the gold award for the President's Physical Fitness Award and of course, the GOLD TEE SHIRT! Fast forward to high school. Late in my junior year I was being recruited to play collegiate football. I was recruited by the University of Miami along with several other universities and was deemed a *BlueChip Recruit*. I ended up being a top-20 recruit in the state of Florida my senior year. I was a part of the Florida High School Association state championship football team that year and later chose to accept a full-ride scholarship to University of Miami. I'll never forget sitting at a table at a big press conference. All the lights were blinding, and I could barely see; all the cameras were rolling, and there I was with the coaches and some of the administrators from the university, signing my scholarship – the first in my family to go to college.

The Real Secret to Top Performance

The point of the story I just told is to outline a few underlying principles of success that have the biggest impact on our results in life. The first principle is that we need to have a goal to strive for. The late personal development expert, businessman and author, Earl Nightingale, said, “Success is the progressive realization of a worthy ideal.” Notice how he didn’t say *accomplishment* of a worthy ideal. Meaning, he defined success on whether we’re striving and working toward something, not the achievement. That green wall for me was a specific, tangible obstacle I had to overcome in order to achieve the outcome I so desired; earning the gold tee shirt and the President’s Physical Fitness

Award. In my mind's eye, I knew exactly what it would look like to climb over that wall. I also knew exactly what type of training I had to place myself through in order to win.

So, what is your goal? What are some of the objectives you want to strive toward right now? Think about them in more than just the terms of business. Think about your goals in every area of your life: financial, health, relationships, business and spirituality. Have you been putting off a dream vacation with your family? Or maybe you have an idea for an art project that you've been avoiding? Did you used to play music in a band, but never found the time to reconnect with your music? Work toward it. Think about what you want to accomplish and start making it happen. *Choose and it will happen.* I learned this from one of my teachers and mentors, Ilchi Lee. Without choosing and without clarity, there is only a wish or a dream. There is beauty in striving for something bigger in your life. You get to experience how your actions create the world around you. Did you know you have that power; the power to create your environment? Yes, you do. By choosing and taking action you are able to experience the flow of success, which builds your confidence.

Another principle for you to consider is questioning to what degree you have a *beginner's mind.* What I mean is: knowing that you *don't know* everything about a topic keeps you curious to learn more. When you're learning, you're growing. On the other side, if you think you know everything, you're less powerful. You don't strive. You don't work through the burn when it's hard. You'll find it's easier to throw in the towel and give up. See, when I first started playing football, I knew I didn't have any idea about how to be a good football player or even a good collegiate player. I knew I had an idea of how to *play,* but didn't know how to be the best. As a result, I listened to my coaches. When they said to do something, I did it. When they yelled at me for making a mistake, I didn't get bitter, I got better. Through enough time, energy and effort, I earned that scholarship. Think about what your goals are and then ask yourself, "How much more can I learn about this topic?" On a scale of one to ten, how teachable are you? I've seen hundreds, if not thousands of people, both in sports and business get too full of themselves, get complacent with practice and ultimately fade off into the background because someone else took their place. Don't be one of those people. Be curious. Think about how much more you can learn. More importantly, seek guidance. I have several mentors and teachers. Do you have a mentor? Is there someone who is massively successful and who you aspire to be like? Someone you can learn from? Make sure you're watching the trainings, reading the books and listening to interviews with successful people on your topic. Make sure you're always actively learning more. That is what *Beginner's Mind* looks and sounds like. Empty your cup so you have space to fill it with a new way of thinking about the world.

The third and final principle I'd like to share about the "underlying principles of success" is probably the most impactful in terms of the immediate and long-term results it produces. This single secret is, in my opinion, the most critical element for you, me, or anyone else to develop if we want to succeed. That single advantage is a type of mindset called *Master's Consciousness*. In the next chapter we'll explore the different components of this type of mindset and skill.

Developing a *Master's Consciousness*

Many years after my football career, and years after discovering the benefits of Tai Chi and Mindfulness, I was researching all sorts of different material on the topic of spirituality and personal development. Since I don't consider myself to be naturally *intuitive* I prefer learning about things I can apply in the business world. One of the concepts I found useful was the *Five Levels of Leadership* in the book *Mastering Leadership,* by Robert J. Anderson and William A. Adams. In it, Anderson and Adams write about how leaders develop through a series of sequential stages. Transformative change requires moving from one level to the next by the leader, the organization and its stakeholders, too. A shift in the culture of the organization to a higher level of development – which I call higher consciousness – is necessary to truly lead and execute effectively in the vastly volatile, uncertain and complex world we live in. The authors refer to *leadership* and the stages of leadership ranging from "*Egocentric" to "Unitive".* When I think of these levels of leadership, I think of them in terms of *levels of consciousness.*

As children, and during our adolescence, we receive everything from the outside. We're dependent on our family to sustain us – completely *at effect* to the world. It's all about "me" at this level. That is the first level. Then we get to early teenage years and early adulthood and we learn that to get along we must go along. We want to fit in and we shape our behavior to meet the expectations of others. We are defined by what others think. It's when we begin looking for acceptance from the outside inward. We're concerned about how "they" perceive us. How do I look to other people? Do I fit in? Our deepest fear is being ostracized or shunned by the group. That's the second level. The third level of consciousness (leadership) happens when we begin shedding assumptions that we've carried with us and that have shaped our lives to that point. At this level we ask questions like: "Who am I?" "What do I care about most?" At this level our inner awareness and acceptance is enhanced, which results in more creativity and wanting to help others. We are more independent and self-authoritative. It's not just about me; I want to help others. Then there's the fourth level, which is the level of consciousness where we think not only creatively but also of the impact decisions have on the diverse stakeholders of the organization. At this stage we are more visionary and understand the complexity of the systems within the organization. The fifth level I call the *Master's Consciousness level.* It's when we're thinking about the bigger picture, striving to make changes that will impact the world, not just us and the ones we're close to. All of us go through various levels. We may go in and out of some of these levels during the course of our lives. Some of us continue to progress, and some of us get stuck in certain levels. We need to look inwardly and have an awareness of where we are on those levels and accept where we are. We're not perfect, and that's okay. Yet, we can choose what we want to do with our lives that matters. It's your life as a leader, how do you want to lead? It's really about being in touch with your heart. We could call the effect of having a *Master's Consciousness* being a heartfelt leader. Can you move beyond that traditional paradigm of "me" and move to the new paradigm of "we"? You have employees, their families, customers, local communities, and the larger world communities. How can you act in a way that brings positive impact to all those people? As a leader in business with a *Master's Consciousness*, your leadership style becomes more heartfelt and authentic. You don't need to save the world. It can be as simple as actively listening to an employee or direct report in your company or organization and helping them find a solution to their problem, or offering a nugget of sage advice. I believe that leading from *a Master's Consciousness* enables you to be the best version of yourself.

How Consciousness Affects Your Body

There is also some very compelling research that illustrates the amazing power of our consciousness as it relates to our ability to succeed. Back in the nineties Dr. David

Hawkins wrote a book called *Power vs Force, the Hidden Determinants of Human Behavior*. He used kinetics (body) tests to create what he called a "map of consciousness." His goal was to help humans evolve by helping them "overcome the inherent limitation of the human mind, whereby falsity has been misidentified as truth." Essentially, Dr. Hawkins's theory was that emotions send out a certain amount of energy. Like a light bulb hooked to a dimmer switch, emotions like *guilt* and *shame* are low and dark on that energy scale, and emotions like *love* and *peace* are bright, and therefore higher on that energy scale. Dr. Hawkins even plotted a certain number to quantify how powerful each emotion is. The numbers scale from zero, at the very bottom, all the way up to one thousand at the top. The emotion at the bottom is *shame* and the top is *enlightenment*. He also lectured that our physical bodies serve as a sort of measuring stick that quantifies the amount of energy of each emotion. Meaning, he demonstrated the level of energy that different emotions have by testing the physical body's strength or weakness in response to those emotions. These kinetic tests are also called *muscle testing,* and when used properly, they can serve as a powerful tool for people to create the life they want without using manipulation or control to do so.

Create Your Ideal Company Culture

Have you ever studied a flock of geese flying in formation? There's a reason why they fly that way. It makes it easier for the whole flock to move forward because they're lifting each other up. Each goose is improving the aerodynamics of the whole group. Also, one goose doesn't always lead the formation. They take turns; enabling one to go to the back to rest and another to lead. I've always found a flock of geese to be interesting as metaphor for effective leadership. In this chapter I'd like to give you eight principles that will help you become a more effective leader. As you apply these principles, you'll find that you and your team function like a flock of geese heading in the same direction. Here they are...

69

Listen Like Your Life Depends on it

Listening is such a basic human skill, yet few people master it. Most people do not give their full attention to whomever they're speaking with. When you listen to people with your full and absolute attention, you're showing them how important they are. Remember: in every person's mind, *they* are the most important person in the world. Appeal to their nature. Give them the gift of your attention. When you listen to a person, you're also helping him or her increase their self-esteem. The psychotherapist, speaker and author, Nathaniel Branden, defined self-esteem in this way: *"The disposition to experience oneself as competent to cope with the basic challenges of life and as worthy of happiness."* Branden also taught that anxiety, depression and relationship challenges happen to the extent a person lacks self-esteem. One of the ways you can help people build their self-esteem is by giving them your full attention. You're giving them space to communicate. This builds trust with them. If you have a trusting organization, everybody feels like they've got each other's back and they're supporting each other, and they're all moving in the same direction. When we listen to others fully and actively we expand the arena where trust is built.

Illuminate Your Blind Spots

As a leader, if you are not being your best self, I bet that most everybody around you is not being their best self either. Remember: *everything flows from you*. What happens in our society is we look on the outside of ourselves for the resources to accomplish what we want. When you demonstrate your best self, your level of energy goes up dramatically because you have a deeper sense of awareness with each person. There's a technique called the *Johari Window*. It was created back in the fifties. You can find it all over the Internet and I've adapted it to my workshops. The exercise is focused around helping people expand their awareness, open the lines of communication and see their own blind spots, while revealing their strengths. We keep a part of ourselves hidden, and there's part of us we let others see. There are some things that others see in us that we don't see, and that's our blind spot. The more we expand that consciousness and close out the façade, the more everyone acts from a place of their best self. The façade is the area which is known by me but not known by you, something that I keep hidden. Everybody has blind spots that others see clearly. When you have a trusting relationship, like with your best friend, they're going to point out your blind spots. If you feel enough trust with the individuals you're working with, they can give you feedback that makes you a better performer. You also build a relationship, and you feel more comfortable reciprocating. If someone has a blind spot or something they could do to improve, feel free to share without judgment to make everybody better – to make the organization better.

Have Zero Tolerance for Passive Aggression

Some people climb the corporate ladder even if it means climbing over people's backs to do so. What creates a passive aggressive response is the desire for control when we feel threatened. We perceive some threat to our physical health or a threat to our ego. In an ego state of mind, it's all about "me." I want control and recognition. If that attention is at stake, our ego dives into all sorts of negative patterns, grasping onto anything that will give it control. People in that state often cannot be their best self. They're really acting from their ego self. Our best self is our true, authentic self. When we get the ego trying to control, we start fearing because the ego recognizes the limited nature of time. In other words, we're anticipating something in the future, and therefore we have anxiety about it. Whereas when we're in that state of awareness, bringing ourselves back to our bodies, we realize we can't control everything and we're not limited. We speak our minds and get out of the "me versus them" pattern because we have a more objective view of the world. It's important to first demonstrate zero passive aggression in your own behavior as a leader. You do this by speaking your mind. You speak your mind best when you first get in touch with your body and remain in the present moment. That way, you can speak your mind in a non-judgmental and non-threatening way. Demonstrate an authentic leadership pattern and you'll notice other people will model it. Never allow passive aggression to sneak into your company's culture.

Set Clear Boundaries

Once you've mastered your ability to make requests and direct people without being passive-aggressive or domineering, only then can you transfer that skill to your team. When you do transfer that skill, you need to set clear boundaries and ensure you enforce them. You can see this in children. If you set rules and the kids violate them, you must say something. If you let them slip, they'll never respect your rules. You're tolerating that behavior. At the lowest common denominator, culture is defined by the actions and behaviors of your team, the expectations you set and the behaviors that you tolerate. Another way to think about culture is that it's also defined by what you acknowledge, appreciate and recognize publicly and on the spot when your people do something good. You want to reward and recognize when people are honoring what's important to you and the organization. Be authentic about it.

When you're avoiding having difficult conversations, you internalize that and it distorts again into "me against them." Then, the only way you can get a little micro bit of control is to send out a nasty comment or all other sorts of finger-pointing. Instead, encourage your people to be great. Teach them to see the greatness in others. Teach them to speak up. Some of the greatest entrepreneurs, business people and leaders surround themselves with good people, people who have talents. They find people that have skills that complement theirs. They're not threatened by having talented people around them. Set your boundaries and enforce them if they're broken. Better yet, have your team participate in defining the behaviors and actions that are consistent with the culture. Defining your culture with your team is an empowering experience. This will give you a new sense of confidence and clarity.

Be Authentic and Give Praise

I was recently interviewed for the podcast CEO Exclusive Radio and the host asked me, "What happens when an executive or CEO goes off, loses their cool or starts yelling at somebody?" I said whatever behavior you want to see from your team, you need to demonstrate that behavior to them. If he or she wants to create a culture of collaboration and trust, yet they lose their cool, they must immediately own their actions. They must apologize appropriately to whoever was affected by it. Some people have really struggled with owning up about their behavior. I've been one of them. I remember having a team meeting with key people in our organization. I was relatively new to the office and had yet to build strong relationships with the people there. A senior manager said something I didn't agree with during the meeting and I began to ask questions in a way that confronted him and humiliated him in front of the group. I didn't mean to, it was an incorrect choice of words this man took offence to. He came to my office upset. When we got back from break, I publicly apologized to the group. I then also praised the senior manager for the courage he demonstrated by coming to my office. The whole experience was positive because it demonstrated to the team that their opinions mattered and the courage to speak up is rewarded. That experience inspired a better culture. Implement this tip by owning your actions if you're in the wrong and praising people when they are doing good work.

Close *The Awareness Gap™*

Carl Jung wrote, "Who looks outside, dreams. Who looks inside, awakens." In seminars I run with companies, I do an exercise called *The Awareness Gap™*. There's a chart, and on the left side, I have them reflect on a moment when they were being their best selves and write down words that describe how they felt in that moment (Remember our exercise earlier? This is another way to energize your team). I actually write all the words from the group on a whiteboard. Then I have them repeat the words. The overall energy-level of the group increases. Then we continue the process reflecting on words that describe a moment in time when they were their worst self and have them write down the negative words that describe how they felt in those moments. Many times, what happens is people have more negative words. I point that out to them. We list the words and everyone says them aloud as a group. Noticeably, the energy level goes down. I further demonstrate the power of our self-talk, positive and negative, through the kinetic approach I wrote about earlier used by Dr. David Hawkins. The result is impactful. I say, "OK, now for yourself, what percentage of the time are you your best self, versus your worst self?" That question helps people become aware of the ways they can improve, thus closing the awareness *gap*. This exercise is often revelatory. People gain a lot from it. In the *Additional Resources* I included a video training on *The Awareness Gap*.

Demonstrate and Reward Courage

If you'll recall the experience I had with the managing director. I gave him praise for acting courageously. Courage is something to be praised. Look for it in yourself and acknowledge it in others. Inspire a "courage culture" within your company. Courage does not always feel good. You risk your acceptance. You may ask, "Will my ideas or my actions be accepted?" It's important to be vulnerable to get to the other side. That is a green wall; like that one I had to climb over in the obstacle course. There was a physical obstacle in my life – that green wall – and it took a year and a half to master that obstacle course and get over that wall. It made all the difference in my life. It took courage for me to say, “I'm not going to live in a way that is not authentic; there's more to me than where people are trying to put me.” And so that thought of “I'm going to earn that award and climb that wall,” that’s where I stepped into my master’s consciousness. It became effortless with practice once I learned how. I just had to keep at it and continually challenge myself. There are so many areas of life where courage can show up. Whenever you know something is right, true and authentic – yet you also feel the fear attempting to prevent your action – you need to face that and overcome it. You need to confront it like a dragon and take it out. Move through the fear and act. That is the nature of courage. Act fast. Don’t contemplate and overthink about it. Just move. Again, allow your connection to your body be at the forefront of your conscious awareness. *Be in your body* within those moments of courage.

Speak From Your Heart

This really fits within my point on passive aggression. One of the biggest issues I've noticed is that people don't speak their truth. They're afraid to speak out about something they feel is important. One of the most impactful experiences in my football career was when a fellow player said, “Fenton, your problem is that you think too much.” I replied, “Got it.” So I stopped thinking during gameplay and started *playing*. In other words, I remained in the moment. As an athlete, you have to be totally in the present moment because if you're not, you're going to get crushed. If my teammate didn’t speak up, then I would have remained blind to that. People tend to hold back for whatever reason. They either fear being ostracized or some sort of retribution. It takes courage when you have a gut feeling that you need to say something or do something that's contrary to the culture. If you don't say anything, then you're holding back, and maybe holding other people back. It happens a lot in group settings and meetings. People don't have the courage to call out the behavior that needs to be dealt with. You can do it in a professional way. Some people can only give praise, and they can't call something out, but other people can't give praise because it takes courage for them to give praise. As a managing partner, sometimes I would think, "Should I praise this person for the job they did or are they going to get a big head, and then performance goes to hell." What was I thinking? By the same token, we didn't get a whole lot of praise; it was normal to get told, "Here's your evaluation; here are the things you need to work on." and that's it. A big part of our culture is we don't praise ourselves enough internally and we tend to not praise others easily. We don't acknowledge ourselves and we don't forgive ourselves enough. And the same holds true for others.

You've got to trust your employees and they must trust you. The first way to gain trust within a team is to first *trust yourself*. If you don't trust yourself and don't trust your instincts, you're not going to trust other people. This is creating a culture where people can’t freely voice their concerns. In a high-trust organization, when your employees have a real concern, they feel that there's a space for them to speak up. They feel empowered to take action; they’re in a culture where that's recognized, acknowledged and appreciated.

Master the Eight Principles of Successful Company Culture

Make a conscious choice to master these principles within your company:

1. Listen Like Your Life Depends on it
2. Illuminate Your Blind Spots
3. Have No Tolerance for Passive Aggression
4. Set Clear Boundaries
5. Apologize & Praise
6. Close *The Awareness Gap*™
7. Demonstrate Courage
8. Speak From Your Heart

In the *Additional Resources* I'm including a printable pocket card with all Eight Principles of Successful Company Culture for you to keep these in mind.

Phase Three: Empower

Create a Whole New World

The *Empower Phase* is the result you attain from your work within the *Energize* and *eXecute Phase.* When you energize your body and mind for the present moment, you're able to execute your top priorities in a way that *empowers* your life and the people around you. Think of it like a cycle that continues for life. Allow this process to stay with you.

In my experience as a managing partner and executive leadership coach, I've been exposed to some of the world's top performing people and teams on earth. These organizations are effective at bringing in revenue and profit, managing projects and people – while still maintaining high levels of personal morale within the culture. On the opposite side, my experience has also exposed me to ineffective teams with piecemeal sales/management systems, poor teamwork skills and company cultures that are filled with passive aggression and low morale. As a result of my exposure to those types of teams there is absolutely no doubt: the thing that separates the professionals from the amateurs is the combination of *mindsets* AND *tactics*. It wouldn't be practical for a salesperson, manager or CEO to do yoga all day and expect their company to grow. We have to develop our mindset *and* use the mechanisms to create results in our business. Remember: *being a productive person in the business world does not mean you have to sacrifice health, family time, happiness or sanity.*

In order to best implement these skills, there are a couple of things that I recommend or encourage people to do now. The first thing is to follow the principle of the Power of

Accumulation. *The Power of Accumulation* says that with consistent practice, daily deposits build upon each other and expand. Think of it like compound interest. The more you deposit and accumulate, the more you will have to draw from in the future. Have some sort of routine for the techniques I've suggested here, and don't beat yourself up if you get off track. Like I said, the *EXE formula* is a cycle. If you miss a day or two, or you forget to get present with your body, it's OK. A routine helps you build up momentum over time. Five minutes in the morning, five minutes in the evening is great. Anytime you're starting to feel stressed, remember the Five-Minute Shifts. You can go back to the *Energize* section at any time and read them, or get the audio versions in the *Additional Resources.* Also, stretch that time out if you like. There is *only* an upside to deep breathing, mental focus and intentional grounding! There is absolutely no downside to these techniques. In my personal routine, sometimes I only have time for five minutes. Yet sometimes I practice these techniques for an hour, incorporating Tai Chi and yoga movements and postures for a more complete experience.

During one of my workshops, someone asked if I could recommend a really good app for meditation. It dawned on me that you were born with the best app you could ever have – your body. Your body is always in the present moment, but your mind could be 1000 different places – in the future, in the past, not totally focused on the present moment – so use your body.

I love to use physical movement of the body. I suffered from anxiety when I was younger. I think that's why I excelled in sports: I got so exhausted from practicing, I could sleep at night. I didn't know this at that point in time, but I was using my body to calm me down. For children with autism, physical activity helps them to calm their brains down and calm their bodies down.

I like to incorporate some physical activity before I do my meditation. If you feel you don't have enough time, then simply focus on your breathing. Count from 10 to zero, breathing in through your nose and then out through your mouth. At times, this is enough.

Consider incorporating *mindfulness moments* in your workplace. *Aetna Insurance* has taken mindfulness to a whole new level in that company led by Andy Lee, the chief mindfulness officer at Aetna. According to Andy, "Stress affects all companies. Mindfulness is an effective way to provide people with the tools to help manage their stress." Big companies are doing this. *Why not you and your company?* Bill Ford, the Chairman of Ford Motor Company, and

Jeffrey Weiner, CEO of LinkedIn, practice mindfulness. Bill Ford shared in a 2013 Harvard Business Review article that taking time to meditate each day was critical. “The practice of mindfulness kept me going during the darkest days,” he said. So you too can empower your teams. You can allow them the space to do meditation or other ways to create mind-space. For example, walking in nature or on the corporate campus is an effective way to reset the mind and release tension and stress. Phil Jackson, the famous professional basketball coach for several professional teams, including the Chicago Bulls in the Michael Jordan era, would guide the team through a meditation to help them prepare for their games. So when the pressure was on, they could focus themselves and be totally immersed in that moment. There’s no question these techniques are effective.

Aside from your mindfulness practices, in regard to your company's culture, you can ask a simple question: "On a scale of one to 10, where do you think we are on the trust spectrum, one being terrible, no trust, and 10, outstanding?" We all need to have each other's back, and you can gauge where your team is on that spectrum. Becoming more aware of yourself enables you to show appreciation and acknowledge people for their contribution to the organization. Review the eight principles I shared in the *eXecute* section. Keep executing the moves that make your dreams into reality.

As a leader, you need to step back and give yourself permission to focus for a moment and really connect with yourself. Observe what's really happening. When you think about your organization, where do you want to lead it? Do you have a destination? Sometimes I meet executives who have no idea what their destination is to be very successful; they don't know where they want to go next. Like: “I've accomplished all this stuff, and now what do I do?” So you need a clear idea of a destination, a vision of where you want to get to. It’s being authentic, leading from your heart. There are some people who accept their ability to lead. You are that leader.

Frank Shamrock, a martial arts coach has a principle called “Plus, Minus, Equal.” A *Plus* is someone who’s better than you at a skill; who you can take instructions from. A *Minus* is someone who you’re better than; who you can give instructions to. An *Equal* is someone who is equally skilled that you compete with and improve each other’s capability. As I mentioned earlier, I have several mentors including: Jack Canfield, author of *The Success Principles*™ and co-author of the massively successful *Chicken Soup for the Soul*® series of books; Ilchi Lee, author and teacher and founder of many different programs on the brain/body connection; Joel Bauer, the "Mentor's Mentor" in marketing; and the list goes on. Any topic I want to master, I always have a mentor who can guide me. Do you have yours? If you would like professional mentoring from me personally, or you have a team or group who needs professional advice on higher efficiency, productivity and profitability – make sure you fill out the John J. Fenton application in the *Additional Resources*.

The Wolf Story

In transitioning to close, I'd like to share with you a story that made an impact on my mind and heart. There was a Native American grandfather who shared a story with his young grandson. He said, "My son, there are two wolves inside of us. They're both fighting. The good wolf is courageous, is humble, and cares about other wolves. It is confident. The bad wolf is concerned only about itself. It is narcissistic. It treats others poorly. It's selfish." The little grandson was looking at his grandfather and asked, "Which wolf will win the battle grandfather?" The grandfather looked at him and said, "The one you feed."

Which voice do we feed inside of ourselves? Do we want to be in that angry, narcissistic ego state, or do we want to be at our best self? The techniques I shared with you in this book enabled me to get my life back in a crazy business world full of stress. They enabled me to "feed the courageous, humble, wolf and be a better leader." I share them with you so you can transform any of your stress into clarity and focus, while remaining calm and grounded. You deserve to be stress free and happy.

Do you have just 5 minutes? In a matter of minutes, or even just the amount of time it takes to take one breath, everything can change. Take 5 minutes in the peace and quiet of your home or office and reflect on what matters most to you in your life and what you appreciate most. Be grateful for all that you have and breathe into your gratitude.

I hope you found in this book how to assemble your life within a context of self-care and mental focus so you can manage your team in a way that produces your best results and empowers you to live your life by your design.

Additional Resources

Get access to all the FREE bonus material that comes with *5 Minute Mastery*™ (a real value: $297):

- (3) Downloadable "Five-Minute Shift" Audios you can use to get grounded, focused and energized.
- Video Training: "How to Close The Awareness Gap™: Keys to Team Self-Esteem in Business."
- Bookmark with all "8 Principles of Successful Company Culture."
- Application for John J. Fenton to coach you or your team.

Get Access Now At:

http://JohnJFenton.com/Book-Free-Gifts

About The Author

John J Fenton, CEO, MBA, BMC, is an author, award-winning speaker, coach and mentor, and entrepreneur. Known as a top leadership self-mastery expert, he is the founder and CEO of John J Fenton Executive Coaching, providing One-on-John™ mentoring and leadership training, team leadership training, team building and more for executives, entrepreneurs and professionals, and their organizations. He guides them in how to expand their insights, think differently and achieve more success in their personal and professional lives, living their life by their design.

As a leader in business for over 30 years, John was the managing partner of the Atlanta practice of BDO USA, LLP, the U.S. member firm of BDO International, the fifth largest accounting and consulting firm in the world. He has worked closely with company executives, entrepreneurs and professionals for over 36 years. He is a member of the Forbes Coaches Council and is a certified Vistage Worldwide Speaker and former Vistage Worldwide Coach. John has mentored and guided hundreds of executives through One-on-John™ mentoring, workshops, seminars and retreats.

John is a graduate of the University of Miami and holds a Masters Degree in Business Administration and a Bachelors Degree in Business Administration from there as well, and was recognized with the highest honor attained at UM as a member of the Iron Arrow Honor Society. John earned his degrees while honing his leadership skills as a key member of the Hurricanes Collegiate Football Team, one of the Nation's top collegiate programs. He has been mentored by some of the world's leading experts and has spent over a decade practicing the Martial Art of Tai Chi and mindfulness earning his black belt in Tai Chi. Among his many accomplishments and certifications, John is a certified Brain Management Consultant, healthy life-style coach and master in mindfulness.

For more information, please visit www.JohnJFenton.com.

Made in the USA
Middletown, DE
28 January 2019